BOY

Poems by Sarah Watson

SARAH WATSON

ISBN-13: 978-0692396148

ISBN-10: 0692396144

to the soft hearted boy

(you made me feel so understood)

to the magical boy

(you were unspeakably lovely)

to the first boy

(you don't really deserve a dedication)

to the invariable boy

(you taught me irreplaceable wisdom)

to the loveliest, kindest boy

(you are the safest place i know)

xx

ONE

there's one thought that has kept me up

it knows every corner of my heart

traveling my brain

without rest or stop

it fills my heart with an agony

that is both restless and relentless

i have nothing but this thought

nothing but its stare

it is in my mirror

it is in the faces of strangers

it has been my company on the tired nights

when you are far away

it lies next to me

in the empty space that

i wish you would inhabit

it chokes my throat

swelling my lungs

it makes me gasp for breath

in the warmest sun

it throws me into the sea

with waves crushing my bones

this thought harasses me

yet i don't let go

because it is hope

it is a link to you

it takes me to you

with energy

as if i am a bird

and this thought is the air expanding my wings

i am never separate from you

or your unknowing gaze

this thought is the glue

to everything i wish we could be

when i am walking through the city

with your voice in the surrounding scape

echoing off the bricks and stones

this question slowly catches up and walks beside me

despite the noise and sirens

i hear it clearly whisper its common phrase

"do you love me too?"

TWO

there is a boy

who makes me bleed

with pain

reverie

and everything

in between

i see his eyes in the sun

when it rises and it sets

i hear his voice in the drum

when it stops and it begins

everything he is

is so lovely

THREE

this vivid light came in

through my open evening window

just as i was thinking of you and i

i realized it was you

coming through miles of space

to meet me for just a moment

you came in the form of a ray

shining warmth upon my face

vanishing the shadows around my eyes

and whispering in my ear

"i'm here"

FOUR

i've spent so many hours of my life on you

i told the world how much you meant

to me

all for the sake of your memory

and perhaps a faint hope

that i would forget you quicker

i was faithful to all i hoped you would be

but you tore me down

and ran away

with an urgency

that hurt more than your leaving

the lies you told me

stayed

despite your disappearance

i believed in my worthlessness

because you were the first person

to tell me that's what you saw

you said i wasn't beautiful

in your words

and in your actions

you created a disease

inside of me

it has taken me years to remove it

to forget the night it began

when your words became my tears

and those tears became an illness

rooting itself

deep down in the cracks

of my skin

heart

and mind

i had this misconception

that i was the problem

that i wasn't enough

but now

looking back

less cracked

and somehow more myself

i see it for what it was

a lie

litter

coming from your mouth

there was no disease inside of me

the disease was your derision

you were the problem

a problem

i couldn't seem to disconnect from

but i'm okay now

time will do that to you

your voice no longer dictates my self-worth

i am free of you

and it is marvelous

FIVE

i see you there
waiting for me among the stillness
your eyes are dark
and your mouth is still

i wait a moment and watch you
as the sun rises behind your face
your breathing is calm
and your silhouette strong

i approach you with a slow walk
gazing with eagerness and a full heart
your smile emerges
and your hand extends

over creeks and valleys we climb
unafraid of what we might find
your motions are kind
and your steps are sure

here with you

i am unafraid

SIX

don't tell me something i've heard a thousand times

tell me something new

like how the sun looks when it rises

among the lofty jungles of vietnam

tell me of your first love

and what kind of man she made you

tell me of the family vacations you took

when you were small and still afraid of snakes

tell me how many times you've wished

you'd find me at your local café

and tell me how you felt

when it finally happened

on that cold december day

tell me what it feels like

to be secure in yourself

to walk down the street

unafraid of what people might think

tell me what you want to name your kids

when you grow up someday

when you decide you're ready

to teach a young mind

how to think

behave

and pray

tell me how many times

you've wanted to die

then tell me why

you decided you wanted to live again

tell me why i matter to you

why i'm the girl you want to see

every morning and every night

before and after sleep

tell me where i can go

when i'm completely missing you

when tomorrow feels like too much

tell me a safe place i can rest

tell me where i can find your eyes

when you've finished with this

and i know everything there is to know

tell me you'll never leave me

because really

that's all i've ever wanted to hear

SEVEN

stevie nicks understands

singing through my car radio

with haunting words like

"i've been afraid of changing

cause i've built my life around you"

what happens if it doesn't work with us?

i never thought that was a possibility

i assumed that once we loved each other

we'd never stop

but people change

don't they?

people move on

they develop different ideas

especially when they're as young as we are

i'm not sure i can live without you

i don't know how to move on

i get stuck

on you

on our life

on everything we create together

if it disappears

it's as if i disappear

maybe that means i've put too much of myself into you

maybe i need to be more myself

and less of you

i think back of all the men i've loved

and all the women you've poured your heart into

we still hold pieces of them

don't we?

even when we're together

their voices echo in our ideas and opinions

because they shaped us

just like you shape me

even if we end

you'll still be a part of me

forever

and this helps me go on

despite the bleeding

our separation would bring upon me

i believe in the influence

your heart can have on mine

and the eternal importance of that

EIGHT

save me with your dark eyes

save me with your kind heart

with your caring and gentle touch

that i can never feel enough

save me with your forgiveness

save me with your understanding

with your endless and sincere love

that has captivated my heart

save me from the cliques

save me from the pain

from the judgments and assumptions

i can never seem to bear

save me from the disdain

save me from insincerity

from the crutches and band-aids

that hide all the scars we still obtain

save me from the world

save me from the ending

let's run away to the place

we will never feel afraid

NINE

oddly enough

i feel rather strong

like perhaps i'm pretending

and i've already moved on

these months of loving you

have felt like seconds

i've been captivated and lost

and the time has vanished

you've taken me far

encouraged me

and lightened my heart

the dreams that were built

encompassed me

they were beautiful

and upright

but now they are done

and i often wonder

whether my affection

seemed foolish to some

it's ironic that i'm okay

because i was always so scared

of life without you

but i know the bravery

that is surging within me

was meant to be

the thread has been sewn between us

through all we have done together

it was a beautiful time

a masterpiece

this journey

you have walked

with me

this gives me strength

to move on

the joy

and the knowledge

that you were the best choice

i have ever made

TEN

you gave me a key
i cried with joy
because i knew
it was the source
to so so much
i hung it from my neck
so as to always
always remind you
that i would never stop
seeking the truth
living inside you

ELEVEN

the sun doesn't rise

until you open your eyes

i'm caught by surprise

at how bright they shine

shadows play on your back

as we lie on the ground

i think of all i might lack

had we never said hello

TWELVE

i have a dream for us

it's filled with beautiful light

we are not scared of crashing waves

or the darkness of the night

i have a dream for us

there's a house of imperfect love

the roof is made of glass

so we can always feel the sun

i have a dream for us

we have dancing feet and lungs

they carry us for hours

as we sing and run in love

i have a dream for us

our garden is full of blossomed fruit

the trees that surround our house

grow strong and tall and true

i have a dream for us
it's full of selfless love
our time is spent re-giving
the hope once given to us

i have a dream for us
full of foggy morning skies
full of coffee mugs and newspapers
which awaken our sleepy minds

i have a dream for us
it speaks of ocean wanderings
there are waves which wet our faces
and preserve our honesty

i have a dream for us
there are children who we have made
and faces not like our own
but our hearts are all the same

i have a dream for us
full of photographs and maps
detailing places we have traveled

that have filled the empty gaps

i have a dream for us
one where you are strong and sure
you pray for our well-being
with a heart that's evening pure

i have a dream for us
one in which we don't compare
our sorrows or our joys
to those beyond our share

i have a dream for us
where i am patient and kind
where you hold me steadily
and tell me "you are mine"

THIRTEEN

i know there is a different girl

and i heard she lives

in your house with you

and i'm so glad

that you are so happy

but i guess i just wish

it was me

FOURTEEN

that feeling returns

a subtle ache of oncoming pain

it starts in your throat

descending slowly down

until it reaches your heart

and suffocates your lungs

it grows into an overwhelming force

violently shaking your body

back and forth

screams and shivers

it won't be quenched

until it finally fades

probably years from now

under a shy morning sun

somewhere far away

where the memory of him

only settles

because

you

finally

found

someone

new

FIFTEEN

my mind is wandering down paths unseen

i see your smile through the sheltering trees

you walk beside me and we hear a song

that binds our hearts in

undying love

the woods grow silent

watching us as we walk

the dark skies above

swell like our thoughts

someday soon

the sun will rise

and all will be clear

SIXTEEN

i can see your eyes
past the rim of your glasses
your skin is brown
under the dim porch light
i can see your loving face
as your lips speak my name

your eyes have faded now
your skin has become old
but your face is no less loving
and my name is still on your lips

you say
"blue, i love you"

SEVENTEEN

i wish my heart didn't feel so much

it makes it hard to be free

there's a heaviness inside me now

because you refuse to leave

even after a thousand tears

your voice still stings my veins

i remember your eyes

and how they shone so kind

but now when i see them

they make my body collapse

grief

i had never felt so understood before

so comfortable and sure

but you kept moving forward

to a place i wasn't allowed to go

i often wish i just had a chance

to make a decision

yes or no

EIGHTEEN

if i have to take down all of your photos

and remove your name from my diluted heart

i will

if i have to stop dreaming of you

and refrain from softly speaking your name

i will

if i have to stop holding your hands

and forget what it feels like to touch you

i will

if i have to stop taking your calls

and find another family to spend the holidays with

i will

if i have to stop wearing your beanie

and donate your old nike sweatshirt

i will

if i have to stop texting you in the morning

and start making my own dinner plans

i will

if i have to stop sending care packages when you're on the road

and forget all of your favorite songs and books

i will

if i have to longboard home alone after work

and get frozen yogurt by myself

i will

if i have to unimagine our lives together

and halt my ideas of destiny and forever

i will

if i have to adopt children alone

and raise them lovingly and without you

i will

if i have to be my own

on my own

and disconnect myself from you forever

i will

but i will not forget the goodness

you never ceased to show

and the way you made me feel

like i was the whole world

standing right in front of you

i will not let your absence

make my life darker

i will grow

and i will become

all i need to be

to be a good daughter

sister

friend

mother

and a good human being

i will be everything i was

when i was with you

because you made me my best

NINETEEN

your eyes take me somewhere

i've never been before

to a cavern of secrets

you keep all to yourself

the only way there

is through a portal

in your pupils

glistening and transporting

you're so afraid

to let me get lost there

so anxious i'll reject what i find

but let me tell you this

and listen close

nothing you have ever done

or will do

could sway me away

from your grace

and magnetism

i promise you that i am here

i am present

i am with you

i'm not afraid

of your faults

or failures

because

i believe in you

your secrets reveal so much

but ultimately

they show me

your face

in a new light

they show me

your heart

in its purest

rawest

most troubled form

and it is everything

i have ever wanted

TWENTY

i talk to you

i laugh with you

i read to you

i smile at you

we go for walks

hand in hand

we sit together

and talk of plans

i trust in you

i believe in you

i wake

i'm jilted into reality

with the remembrance

that you are not here

anymore

suddenly

i'm cold

my hands feel empty

my voice goes quiet

i'm alone

without you

and

it

hurts

TWENTY-ONE

the first mile was suffocating

as i left the parking lot

and pulled away from the place

i knew you were to stay

driving by cars

skyscrapers

and endless crowds of people

i only thought of you

every turn of my car took me

further

and

further

away from your light

and i hated that

i replayed every moment of leaving

every small

torturous task

key in ignition

reverse

right blinker

tick

tick

tick

look back

no sign of you

drive on

the feeling

the sickening

literal heart ache

i felt as though i would explode in the worst way

my heart kept growing inside of my chest

swelling and attacking

but i couldn't let it out

because the whole world was watching

i couldn't say a word

so i just drove

mile

after

mile

away

from

everything

i

loved

TWENTY-TWO

goodbye my dear

sweet sailing to you

i wish you well

as you depart

from my crying mind

and exhausted heart

the air is frigid

and my body is shivering

thinking of the oncoming cold

and from here on

how i must go alone

frozen

confused

paralyzed

as you float away

i close my eyes

i can't watch you go

so i reminisce

of sweet memories

in the back of my mind

hoping the thoughts

will strengthen my bones

but knowing nothing can shatter

the honest truth

i am alone

farewell sweet boy

farewell

for the rest of time

TWENTY-THREE

i promise you

all of these words mean something

i'm just not sure what

give me some time

i'll come around

i'm just not sure

who i am yet

my focus is tilting

and my steps are unsteady

if i knew what to do

then i don't think

i would think of you so much

TWENTY-FOUR

i've messed up a lot

i get lost

in the noise

in his eyes

in the ideals of others

it's scary when you realize

that you're slowing fading

and hardly any piece

of who you once were

remains

but i think it's healthy

to forget

at least for a little while

because when you get to the low point

you realize

nothing mattered more to you

than what you had

before

TWENTY-FIVE

i need to tell you something

quickly and simply

i'm so happy

so full of reverie

at the sight of you

and i want you to know

that these untroubled tears

are years of you

some of the best years i've known

you were so genuine

you were the best of men

you took me high

and never let me down

you were my sky

and my solid

steady ground

you shaped me

changed me

and it was exactly what i needed

thank you

starry eyed boy

TWENTY-SIX

i wish it wasn't ending now

right before winter

when the world loses all of its life

and i have to fight to survive

i can't face the cold

lifeless months

that are about to hit me

without your safety

if i'm going to make it

i'll need springtime

the promise of new life

i need warmth

and a new kind of green

but every time i look outside

with only you on my mind

i see falling leaves

and it smothers me

the world is going to sleep

as you are being removed from me

how does one breathe

in times like these?

nothing happens

when i try to inhale

so i am left

on the stormy nights of autumn

gasping for air

and for a promise

and for you

with every step you take

away from my face

i grow whiter

and more faint

i'm so afraid

of going on without you

i see you in everything

how am i supposed to forget

when you are in the tree

growing by my window?

when you are the rings

that decorate my fingers?

you are the rain

on my windshield

every sip of coffee

in the lonely afternoons

you are there

all around me

because my life

has only been you

and i am haunted

TWENTY-SEVEN

what if we had met

under a different sun

when you

were younger

and i

was less self aware

TWENTY-EIGHT

i write about you anywhere i can

because i am overflowing with you

i write my notes

on the frosted windows

enclosed between

my bedroom walls

i write poems

that you will never hear

on my thin

weary

and tired skin

words to you can now be found

on city streets

around the world

that i have walked

with thoughts of you

you are everywhere

and thus i cannot escape you

TWENTY-NINE

he builds me

and kills me

he crushes my heart

with his gaze

of summer time

i can't tell if he's the best thing

or the worst thing

to happen to me

but i don't want to let him go

because life without his eyes

grin

step

voice

hands

and heart

sounds unbearable

THIRTY

i love you

and i hope you never change

or give up

on the boyish idea

of optimism and peace

because that's the you

i fell for

back when i was just

learning how to be myself

and you swept in

like an unexpected breath

of fresh air

in a world

where the air

sometimes

doesn't exist

THIRTY-ONE

imagine

the

poetry

you

could

write

if

only

he

loved

you

back.

THIRTY-TWO

things you were

long distance phone calls

saturday night theater dates

never ending rooftop dances

night time car rides

the warmest summer days

my favorite acoustic playlist

things you are now

none of the above

THIRTY-THREE

you have so many versions

and i love them all

but my favorite is you

at home

softly wandering around the green

in your wellies and striped sweater

you look for beauty

that might have been lacking

out beyond the sunrise

of noise and people

you found it there

behind the pines

and beyond the pond

the quiet you needed to recharge

wait for me there

i'll hold your hands

and shield them from the coming winter

we can sit until it's too cold

then we'll run

with burning faces

through the ever changing landscape

until we're out of breath

and warmed inside

perfectly content

with our eyes

and hearts

and lives

these journeys remind us

of who we will become

when we stick together

and put our faith in more

than us

i lean closer

as we walk home

i slowly look at the sky

as you look at me

and we both know

deep down

that we're going to make it

after all

THIRTY-FOUR

i wish i knew how to draw

because then

i could sketch your eyes

on scraps of paper

keeping them in my pocket

or paint them upon my legs

so whenever i'm alone

or in a crowd

or afraid

or tired

or completely

and urgently

in need of you

i could look into the color

of summer

and safety

and

everything

would

be

okay

THIRTY-FIVE

i told them that i had let him go

but that wasn't the truth

he's been hiding inside of my heart

for so long

he won't leave

because we both feel at home

so perfectly at ease

when the rhythm of our hearts

is flawlessly on beat

he is so familiar

i need him

to carry on

THIRTY-SIX

if i could just tell you

how much i long

for your hand

to slip gently into mine

i think perhaps

i'd feel at ease

shake hands

and become friends

with the terrifying idea

of more time

THIRTY-SEVEN

this is how he made me feel loved

when my heart was heavy

and my eyes burned

he said i was strong

and capable

that i would make it through

even when the heaviness

of my previous failures

burned in the lines

of the comments of others

this is how he made me feel loved

when i awoke

with messy hair and smudged makeup

he would look at me

and say

"you are the brightest version

of the morning sun i always

want to see lying next to me

so please never leave"

this is how he made me feel loved

when my dog died

and i could barely speak through the tears

he asked me if i wanted to watch balto

and he wrapped me in a bundle of blankets

so i could cry and feel at home

amongst the sorrow i didn't know

would be so hard

this is how he made me feel loved

when i would run away

and hide for days

he would tell me

my depression did not own me

"it is only a part" he would say

"and the joy is so much bigger

so when you're ready

i'll be right here

waiting to help you come back up"

this is how he made me feel loved

when he would read aloud

my favorite books

so i could lean my chin

against his sturdy shoulders

and feel my favorite words

from my favorite voice

sink into my skin

this is how he made me feel loved

he would tell me about his fears

and his hopes

how they were like colors on the wall

mixing and blending

sometimes overwhelming

he would say how he was sometimes uncertain

but he wanted to be sure

he trusted my wisdom

and i wanted more than anything

for him to understand

how much he meant to me

whether he succeeded or not

this is how he made me feel loved

by completely being in awe

of the minutes and the hours

collected in a day

surrounding us and counting

keeping track of our breaths and decay

how he knew to be present

in a situation where i was restless

this is how he made me feel loved

by being human

with me

by loving God

with me

by trusting me to go along with him

till kingdom come

THIRTY-EIGHT

i'll miss the etched ink
of green and black
upon your skin
like a canvas of who you are
for all to see
adding mystery and certainty

i wish i could capture
your laughter
inside of my throat
so even after this is over
it'll come out of me
and hopefully carry me

we are so young
so unborn in the scope of life
maybe that's why
the lines have been drawn
and i'm on this side
and you're not

maybe when we're both forty-five

and really really alive

we'll meet on a sidewalk

unscathed and unafraid

we'll be happy

for each other

and share a hug

and carry on

THIRTY-NINE

i feel tepid

not because you're gone

but because you weren't whole

i have nothing else

inside of me

now that i see it

with the eyes

of a girl

who can't be in love anymore

the only thing

i can find to say

is simply

i am so sorry

and sad

FORTY

i could write a different poem

for every picture i see of you

your eyes are magnetic

bright and fierce

producing the most sincere and kind gaze

i have ever felt

your mouth is the moon

shaped just so

speaking life and wisdom

and lighting up the world

you have a radiance

i have never seen

or felt before

FORTY-ONE

my home is so close to yours

we're separated only by ocean

and people's ideas

come stay with me

i'll give you another place to escape to

FORTY-TWO

i want to know what your handwriting looks like

and what scenic picture you would pick out on a postcard

i want to hear you laugh during your favorite movie

and see which ones make you cry and ache

i want to feel the callouses of your hand

and see those hands wave to kids on parade floats

i want to hear your voice when you talk firmly

and i want to hear it when you whisper secrets

i want you to explain your fears and dreams

and i want to know why you love the things you do

FORTY-THREE

paris dreams

live inside of your veins

slow nights

twinkling lights

it's glowing in your eyes

i can see the truth of the world

coming in the beams

of morning sun

as i walk down

the awakening street

after being with you

all night

we talked

of tomorrow

and yesterday

and the things

we've always

been afraid to say

FORTY-FOUR

i love you most

when i'm in brooklyn

because the city makes me forget you

and when i'm less consumed

i'm most in love

the noise overrides

the tiring sound of my doubt

i'm aware of everyone else

and their faults

and suddenly you seem better

my insecurities surrounding you

fade with the sunset

but the possibilities of us

are ever illuminated

like the bright city light

we are a contradiction

one i always seem to handle better

when i'm in brooklyn

FORTY-FIVE

i can't really tell you

how badly it hurts

to finally realize

i'll never

get to hold your hand again

how the separation

will turn your gentle

patterned arms

into a memory

i'll never again

be able to feel around my waist

FORTY-SIX

sometimes i hear people say really basic words

and i remember how you say it

with your deep

and slow moving voice

a flood of you comes back to me

and i am a mess of tears and joy all at once

you are my ribcage and my heartbeat

everything you do

is in rhythm with my step

when your hands touch

i feel

what your mouth speaks

i have thought

we are the same

you and i

we are glued together

by our mirrored understanding

of the world

of people

of love

FORTY-SEVEN

i love you because you are the man who hugs his mum every day

i love you because you are the man who isn't afraid to go forth
when others shy away

i love you because you are the man who looks beyond the cliché

i love you because you are the man who doesn't define by the body
but by the heart

you are good

even though good is impossible

you are still good

and it amazes me

i love you because you are the man who notices the kid in the corner

and you make that kid feel infinite

FORTY-EIGHT

i can't move on

because you are the goodness

i've been searching for

in a crowd of disbelief

FORTY-NINE

favorite times

staying up late

with you

listening to jazz

talking of california

and the day

we'll finally get there

feels so good

so home like

to live inside

of your mind

and eyes

can't go to sleep

because you

are magic

in front of me

can't see life

without you

cause you

have stolen me

not a slave

anymore

to the idea

of being alone

cause you're here

and billie holiday

keeps playing

all night long

like a sweet reminder

that you're not

leaving

FIFTY

green

is my favorite color now

because it represents

how you see the world

and how you see the world

is my favorite thing about you

FIFTY-ONE

they say

"how do you write this

where does it come from?"

i look at their questioning eyes

and smile as i explain

it's your kindness

and never ending wonder

your burning desire for life

and awareness of others

these things light me up

they set me ablaze with affection

i walk away breathless

after having talked of you

for so long

there is no air left in me

so i float away to the sky

to live among the stars

this is where you wait for me

and as i drift above

i hope someday

they have someone too

who makes them feel this much

FIFTY-TWO

i didn't want to tell anyone

about the love

i had for you

i didn't want to tell anyone

about the way

that you made me feel

like a treasure

hidden beneath

removable fear

cause you were the sweetest secret

i'd ever been allowed to hold

and i knew

that the voices of

judgement

and

insincerity

would

try to come in

and poison

the lovely

home we built

between our souls

FIFTY-THREE

it has been so long since i've been enamored by a boy
for years nobody truly caught me
nobody made my heart ache
nobody made me want to run away
but here i am
sitting next to this incredible boy
years of being myself
finally paid off
it's overwhelming
i forgot how consuming it is
how you feel as though
you can never love anyone else
how they are the stars
the moon
and
every inch of night time sky
his arms wrap around me
slowly and surely
and i feel as though i've come home
i watch him read across from me

and the way his eyes react when the words hit him

makes me fall in love all over again

he teaches me to love things

gets me up early to watch the sunrise

he sits quietly in awe

as it makes the world come alive

he is aware of beauty in its rawest form

engaging with children

feeding the homeless and clothing the naked

even on his bad days

he handles himself with grace

slowly walking away from confrontation

yet standing up when words need to be spoken

we ride our bikes to mcdonalds at midnight

and i laugh as he drinks his chocolate shake

and rides over the boardwalk singing U2

he doesn't let me win at tennis

because he believes girls

are strong enough to beat boys

and i do win

and he loves it

and i love him

it is beautiful

this world he has created with me

about the author:

sarah watson | 1993 | not looking for perfection | set free by the most beautiful King

connect: sarahxxwatson@gmail.com

twitter & tumblr: sarahxxwatson

many warm thanks to my family and friends for supplying me with kindness and courage, during this project and always.

praise and thanks to Hashem, for giving me breath, and for being my constant safety.

xx